The V

WHIZZ DOME
(full of wisdom)

Ear full of wax

mouthful
of fascinating
information

This book belongs to

..... — ..... — ..... — .....

..... — ..... — ..... — .....

..... — ..... — ..... — .....

Peter Eldin

The Whizzkid's Whizzbook

with drawings by Roger Smith

An Armada Original

The Whizzkid's Whizzbook was first published
in Armada in 1986 by Fontana Paperbacks,
8 Grafton Street, London W1X 3LA
Second impression 1986

Armada is an imprint of
Fontana Paperbacks, part of
the Collins Publishing Group

Printed in Great Britain by
William Collins Sons & Co. Ltd, Glasgow

Contents

Check List for Travellers

A check list does not have to be checked. It can be any colour you like, provided that it is checked. For, if you do not check it it will no longer be a check list. Check!

Actually it is a good idea to make up a check list of all the things you are likely to need on a journey. It is as well to make this list before the start of your travels. If you leave it until you are actually on the move or when you reach your destination it can prove frustrating to then discover that you've left the kitchen sink behind.

Here is a simple check list of things you might need on the journey.

Sunglasses (complete with windscreen wipers in case it rains)

Brochures about the places you plan to visit (you can read them while travelling—unless you are the driver)

Traveller's cheques (to buy things along the way—especially useful in Cheque—oslovakia)

Personal stereo (great for listening to personals)

Tapes and batteries for stereo

Pack of cards (useful if you go by ship and want to play some deck games)

Notepad and pencils

This book (you can also take some other books without offending the author of this one—especially if they are by Peter Eldin)

Phrase book (useful if going to foreign parts like Timbuktu—or Clacton)

Elephant repellant

Camera and films (you never know what may develop during your travels)

Sun tan oil (if travelling in Britain rust remover might be more useful)

Sausages (just in case you get hungry)

Plenty of plastic bags for rubbish

A damp flannel in a plastic bag (great for freshening up during a long journey provided that you take it out of the bag first. It's a good idea to put some Eau de Cologne on the flannel—don't worry, boys, it's not cissy to feel refreshed)

All these items can be carried in a bag or case. A case can be particularly useful as you can put it on your lap and use it as a table if you forgot to bring the dining room table with you (you should have put it on your check list).

Watch the birdie

You Are the Navigator

If you are taking a journey by car with your family appoint yourself Official Navigator. You could even make yourself a cardboard badge with the word 'Navigator' on it so everyone will know how important you are (if they do not know it already).

"But what is a Navigator?" you may ask. Good question—what is a navigator? Let's take a look in the dictionary . . . '*Navigator—worker employed in digging a canal*'. Huh? You are certainly not planning to dig a canal, are you?

Let's look again . . . '*Navigator—a person who navigates*'. That doesn't help much either. So let's look up 'Navigate' and see what we get. Ah, this looks better . . . '*Navigate—to direct the course of a ship or aeroplane*'. No mention of cars but we will assume that cars, elephants, camel trains and other forms of travel are also included.

So that is your job as navigator. You have to tell the driver what directions to take. But how do you know which way to go? That's simple—you ask the driver!

A day or two before the journey sit down with the driver (if you prefer, you can stand up with the driver, it makes no difference to me) and a good map (bet you didn't know maps could sit down!) and you both work out the route you are going to take.

Choosing a route is quite an art in itself. The most direct route is not always the quickest and the quickest is not always the prettiest. The route you choose will depend on possible traffic conditions, the time you want to travel and how quickly you want to reach your destination. When the route has been decided mark it in pencil on your map.

To add to your interest, and to the interest of the other passengers, spend a while looking at the map to see what counties and towns you will pass through and what rivers you will cross.

If you have time before you go, look these up in an encyclopedia to discover if there are any fascinating facts about the places you are going to pass. If there is a special building, ancient monument, old battle site, or other item of interest along your route (or near to it) it may prove worthwhile to go off the main route to take a look.

Now, back to the business of navigating. It is your job as official navigator to tell the driver in advance which roads and turnings to take. So you must know where you are at all times. Keep one eye on the road, one eye on your map—and you can do what you like with the other eye.

In addition to knowing where you are and giving the driver directions, a good navigator keeps an eye (not another one!) open for the signposts and junctions along the route. This is especially important in towns where the driver is concentrating on the road and the actions of other drivers and pedestrians.

Especially important when the driver is concentrating on the actions of other drivers

A good navigator also keeps an eye on the time, an eye on the mileage covered and an eye on the petrol gauge. With all those eyes you need it seems that the only thing to make a good navigator would be a peacock!

Off the Rails

What did the railway traffic controller say when he could not get electric trains for his area?
Diesel have to do.

PASSENGER: A return ticket, please.
CLERK: Where to?
PASSENGER: Why, back here of course!

The guard was about to signal the train to start when he saw a pretty girl standing on the platform by an open door. She was talking to another girl who was inside the carriage.

"Come along, ladies," said the guard. "Please close that door."

"Oh, I just want to kiss my sister goodbye," said the girl on the platform.

"You just shut that door," said the guard, "and I'll see to the rest."

Railway Station Announcement: The train now arriving on platforms six, seven and eight . . . is coming in sideways.

What kind of ears does a train have?
Engineers.

What's the difference between a train driver and a teacher?
One minds the train and the other trains the mind.

PASSENGER: How long will the next train be?
PORTER: About eight carriages, sir.

GUARD: Do you like working on the railways?
DRIVER: It certainly has its points.

RAILWAY POLICEMAN: Why are you standing on this railway bridge with a rod and line?
BOY: I'm waiting to catch the next train.

FIRST PORTER: I had a hard job getting that woman's luggage on the London train.
SECOND PORTER: Why, was it heavy?
FIRST PORTER: No. She wanted to go to Blackpool.

On the Road

Next time you're travelling by car tell your fellow passengers some of these amazing snippets of information. They'll be so fascinated and intrigued by your wealth of knowledge that they'll probably fall asleep (so don't tell them to the driver).

England was the first country in the world to have a white line in the centre of the road. The idea was first suggested in 1843 but it was not until the 1920s that they were used to any great extent.

It has been calculated that in Britain there are 83 cars to every kilometre and a half of road. That's one car every nineteen metres—makes crossing the road a pretty chancy business.

The rickshaw was invented by an American priest in Yokohama in 1869. No, his name was not Rick Shaw—it was Jonathan Scobie.

A man was arrested in Denver, Colorado, USA for stealing spark plugs from cars. When police went to his home they found 290,000 of them! He must have been a bright spark.

Japanese scientists have designed an engine that runs on oil squeezed from tangerine peel. There is just one snag—you need the peel from eleven thousand tangerines to produce just one litre of oil. This works out at over a thousand times more expensive than petrol so it does not seem likely that the idea will ever catch on.

The first traffic lights in Britain were erected outside the Houses of Parliament, London, in 1868. They looked like the "semaphore-type" signals used on the railways, which is hardly surprising for they were designed by John Knight, a railway signalling engineer. They didn't last very long—three weeks after their installation they blew up!

Crossing the Line

If you travel on a ship that crosses the equator you may see the 'Crossing The Line' ceremony. If you are crossing the equator (once described by a whizzkid as "an imaginary lion running around the earth") for the first time you may even turn out to be the victim.

In the traditional ceremony the victim's face is covered with shaving cream and then he is 'shaved' with a large wooden razor (you'd better grow a beard, quick). Then he has to eat some pills (these are usually made of flour). After that he is 'baptized by Neptune' in a tub of sea water.

The ceremony is held in honour of King Neptune, the ancient Roman god of the sea, and his wife Amphitrite who also takes part in the ceremony. It is said that the purpose of this curious custom is to make the first-time equator-crosser into a fully fledged sailor.

Nowadays the baptism usually means that you are thrown into the ship's swimming pool but there is at least one consolation—you receive a certificate stating that you have "Crossed the Line".

How to make a first-time equator-crosser Crosser

YOU HAVE CROSSED THE LINE

Next time I'll go by air

Food for Thought

On your travels you will no doubt be eating from time to time. It's always interesting to sample the traditional foods of the region or country through which you are travelling. Test your knowledge of foreign fare with this quiz and see if you know from which countries these dishes come. To help you, the countries are given on the right—but to confuse you they are in the wrong order! Can you rearrange the list so that each food is with its correct country?

MENU
International Cuisine

Spaghetti Bolognese	Denmark
Roganjosh	Greece
Paella	Italy
Smorgasbord	Russia
Cous-Cous	Spain
Goulash	China
Wiener Schnitzel	India
Bird's Nest Soup	Turkey
Sauerkraut	Mexico
Haggis	North Africa
Tamale	Austria
Shish Kebab	Scotland
Dolmas	Hungary
Borscht	Germany

Lost Property

It is amazing what strange things people lose on journeys. The lost property offices of airlines, railways and bus companies bulge at the seams with all sorts of things. Some items that have been found in a lost property office are listed here. Unfortunately, they have got rather mixed up. Can you unravel the letters and say what each item is?

On the Map

A whizzkid should know the symbols found on maps. Some maps have different symbols but what they are is explained in a table on the map (shouldn't the map be on the table?) The symbols shown on this page are some of those used on ordnance survey maps. The things they represent are listed below. See if you can name each symbol correctly.

CAMP SITE
BUS STATION
CHURCH (WITH TOWER)
CHURCH (WITH SPIRE)
SITE OF A BATTLE

ORCHARD
WINDMILL
POWER LINES
(PYLONS)
POST OFFICE
YOUTH HOSTEL

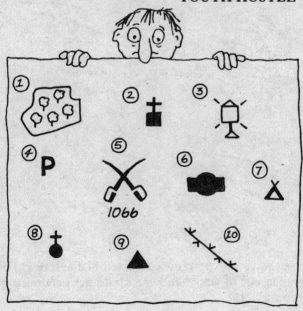

Up, Up, and Away!

These are some of the rules issued to aeroplane travellers by an airline in the 1920s.

Do not touch the propellor.

Do not put your head outside the aeroplane as the force of the wind might surprise you.

the wind is surprisingly forceful

Do not wave your scarf out of the aeroplane. It might be pulled out of your hand and could get entangled in the rudder.

Take a good pair of goggles with you and wear a leather or silk hood.

Keep swallowing during take-off and landing.

Never throw anything out of the aeroplane. Even something small falling from a height of just a few kilometres can attain the speed of a bullet and could prove dangerous to earthly mortals.

Empty your bladder before leaving.

Do not eat such food as peas, beans or brown bread as they are liable to cause the formation of gas in the intestines.

Beans are liable to form gas in the intestines...

Flying Fun

CUSTOMS OFFICER: Excuse me, sir. Why are you standing on your head?

PASSENGER: Because some idiot has stuck my passport photograph in upside down.

A man and his wife arrived late at the airport after a frantic car journey through busy traffic. They rushed up to the barrier with their luggage when the man said:

"I wish I'd brought the piano with me."

"What on earth for?" asked his wife.

"I've left the tickets on it."

Can you telephone from an aeroplane?

Certainly, anyone can tell a phone from an aeroplane.

FIRST PASSENGER: Isn't flying exciting! Look at those people down there, they look just like ants.

SECOND PASSENGER: Don't be silly. They are ants. We're still on the runway.

Two people were standing in the observation area of an airport, when one of them said: "Do you know, I'd hate to be up there in a plane."

His friend looked at him and replied: "Well, I'd hate to be up there without a plane."

Did you hear about the nervous passenger?
He got airsick when he licked air mail stamps.

Did you hear about the aeroplane that was so old it had an outside toilet?

The little old lady was making her first flight and was rather nervous about the idea. The captain walked along the aisle and she stopped him. "Please, captain. You will bring me down safely, won't you?" she asked.

"Don't worry, madam," said the captain. "I've never left anyone up there yet."

No-one has ever complained of a parachute not opening.

Reading between the Lines

Whenever you go somewhere special it's a good idea to get hold of any tourist brochures about the place you are visiting. Holiday brochures make quite interesting reading themselves, but if you are going to choose a holiday from one of them you have to learn to read between the lines for they do not always say exactly what they mean.

For the discerning traveller, here is a list of some of the phrases you will find in holiday brochures. The true meaning is given next to it.

modern, well appointed hotel	*we haven't started building it yet*
hotel overlooking the ocean	*on a stormy day it is in it*

Hotel overlooking the ocean

our hotel is a stone's throw from the beach	*if you are an Olympic discus champion*
bed linen changed every day	*from room to room*
wide range of entertainment	*two juke boxes and a one-armed bandit*

secluded area	*miles from anywhere*
golden beaches	*quicksand*

Golden beaches

secluded area

popular holiday resort	*no-one goes there*
tea like mother makes	*tea that is nothing like the tea that mother makes*
our restaurant serves local specialities	*food you could not possibly eat*

Our restaurant serves local specialities

balmy weather	*barmy weather*
attractive scenery	*if you like looking at factory chimneys*
friendly, reliable staff	*if you give them a big tip*
neat, compact rooms	*the rooms are so small even the mice have round shoulders*

neat compact rooms

friendly atmosphere	*the walls are so thin you can hear everything that is going on in the next room*

27

Signs of the Times

Whizzkids should have no problems in spotting that Peter Eldin does not know his Highway Code very well. His explanations of the meanings of these British road signs are definitely not in the code book. Do you know what they really mean?

1 Camel crossing

2 Watch Out for low flying boomerangs

3 Bottle Bank

4 Car Wash

5 Rain coming

6 Beware! Banana skins on road

Pack It In

Most people have their own way of packing a suitcase. The easiest way is simply to bung everything in and then ask a helpful elephant to sit on the lid while you do up the fastenings.

There are two big problems with the "bung it all in" method. The first is that you usually cannot get everything into the case and the second is that your clothes get so creased you have to spend the first two weeks of your fortnight holiday ironing them.

Here are a few tips for better packing. If you are the lazy type and rely on other people to do the packing show them this page and tell them that you are just trying to be helpful (provided, of course, that you do not have to do any actual work).

Roll up smaller items and use them to fill in the gaps between more bulky items

Open the case first. This makes the job of packing much easier.

Heavy and bulky items such as camel-hair coats (take the camel out first) should go at the bottom of the case. Spread them out as evenly as possible.

Roll up smaller items like underwear, swimming costumes and wooden planks (if you want to keep a log of your trip). Use them to fill in the gaps between the more bulky items.

Don't bundle up your clothes. Fold or roll them neatly to avoid too many creases. After all, you don't want to look scruffy do you? You do? Oh, well—in that case just bung 'em in.

If you are the neat and tidy type and you decide to press some of your clothes before packing (or, better

you may
arrive late

still, get someone else to press them) allow them to air
out for a while before you put them in the case.

Leave night clothes and toiletries near the top of the
case so you can get to them easily. This is especially
important on long journeys where you may arrive late
or if you have to stay somewhere overnight.

If travelling by air do not put any aerosols or fountain
pens in your case for they may leak during the flight.
Never put films in your case either for security x-ray
machines at airports may damage them.

Don't forget your toothbrush. In fact it's a good idea
to make a list of everything you want to take (see page
9). You can then tick each item off the list as you put it
in. Put the list in the case as well—so you will not forget
to bring everything back on the return journey.

Hotel Check-In

The first real hotel was Low's Grand Hotel which was opened at Covent Garden, London in January 1774. Before that time people who wanted to stay in a place for several nights had to rent furnished lodgings or, if the stay was fairly short, stay in an inn.

The largest hotel in the world is the Hotel Rossiya in Moscow, USSR. It is twelve storeys high and has 3,200 rooms and 93 lifts.

Bedrooms in the Hilton Game Lodge in Tsavo Park, Kenya are fitted with elephant buzzers under the beds. It's true! The purpose of these buzzers is not to let you know there is an elephant under the bed. You will know that when your nose is pressed against the ceiling. No, the buzzers are to let you know there is 'big game' in the area so you can go and take a look.

Fancy staying in an elephant? Then try the Elephant Hotel in Margate, New Jersey, USA—the building is shaped like an enormous elephant (or should that be mammoth elephant?). There are staircases in the legs of the elephant that lead to the main rooms.

The Tremont House in Boston, USA was the first hotel to have bathrooms. The hotel was opened on 16th October, 1829 and the eight bathrooms serving some 250 guests were housed in the basement. If you wanted a bath you had to go out of the hotel and into the street and then into the basement through a separate entrance.

At The Residence Hotelière in the Camargue you can stay in bungalows that stand on floating islands of reeds. Great if you like books and want a reed in bed!

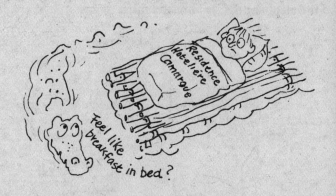

There is a putting green on the roof of The Mandarin Hotel in Hong Kong.

Possibly the most expensive hotel visit in the world would be a day spent in the Royal Suite of the Nova Park Elysées Hotel in Paris. It will cost over £3,500!

Perils of Travel

Most journeys proceed without a hitch. But when something does go wrong strange things can begin to happen—as some travellers found when they went to board an aeroplane in Nigeria. The airline had overbooked and there were three times as many passengers as there were seats on the plane!

It was quite a problem but local soldiers soon solved it—in a most unusual way. They made all the people run around the plane twice. The fastest runners were given the seats!

Seats were also a bit of a problem for some wardens travelling in South Africa's Kruger Game Park. They left their helicopter for a short while, confident that nothing untoward would happen to it. But they were wrong for when they returned they discovered that the seats were gone! A pack of hyenas had eaten them!

It obviously does not pay to leave any vehicle unattended. Jack Carver realized the costly truth of this when his car ran out of petrol in Indianapolis, Indiana, USA. He left the car where it was and went off to get some petrol.

When he returned with the petrol the following day the car still would not go. The reason was quite simple. During his absence the battery had been stolen. There was only one thing to do—he went off to buy another battery. But his efforts turned out to be a waste of time for when he returned to the spot the car was gone!

Even in the sober British Isles there are some strange traveller's tales to relate. In London, for example, two policemen left their police car to investigate an abandoned vehicle. When they came back to their car three of the tyres had been eaten! They later discovered that the perpetrator of this terrible deed was a bull terrier well known in the area as "the tyre-eating terror."

ALLO
ALLO
ALLO

I suspect this is the work of 'the tyre-eating terror'

At least their expense was not so high as that of the British lady who stopped at a garage for petrol and ended up £25,000 poorer. Unfortunately she did not stop at the pump quickly enough and hit a Volvo parked there. The Volvo shunted forward and smashed into a Metro which in turn rammed a BMW that was on show in the forecourt.

This train of events so upset the lady that when she tried to reverse away she used the wrong gear and shot forward and hit the Volvo again. No, this time it did not hit the Metro. It hit another BMW instead—and that crashed into a Mercedes!

Maybe that lady would have been better off if she had travelled by train. But even rail travel can have its problems as some commuters in Britain found out. All the trains had come to a standstill and they were going to be late for work. After a long delay the trains got going again but the irate travellers would have been very surprised if they had been told that the cause of the problem was a mouse!

The animal had appeared in the box of signalman Trevor Hockham. It drove him mad as it scuttled all over the place. Eventually Trevor could stand it no longer so he put all the signals to red, shut up the signal box and went home!

STOP PRESS

BRITISH RAIL SCUTTLED BY MOUSE!

At least the passengers on that occasion reached their destination, which is more than can be said for one American traveller. He decided to take a trip to Italy but ended up in New York by mistake. He booked into a hotel and went looking at the sights of what he thought was Rome. On one occasion he asked a policeman for directions. He asked in Italian of course and, as chance would have it, the policeman was of Italian descent so he replied in the same language. It was not until two days later that the unfortunate traveller discovered that he was still in America!

Places to Visit

It is a good idea for people to go on holiday to places that really suit them. Here are a few suggestions:

ICE CREAM SELLERS
CHILE

POTTERS
CHINA

WALKERS   ROME

FIREWORK MANUFACTURERS   BANGOR

Transport Tangle

All the different types of transport listed below are hidden in the grid of letters on the opposite page. The words may be written forwards, backwards, horizontally, vertically, or even diagonally. One has been ringed to give you a start. Now see if you can find them all.

AEROPLANE

AIRSHIP

AUTOGYRO

BALLOON

BARGE

BICYCLE

BOAT

BROUGHAM

BUS

CANOE

CAR

CHARIOT

COACH

ESCALATOR

FERRY

GONDOLA

HELICOPTER

JET

LIFT

LINER

LORRY

LUNAR ROVER

PEDICAB

RAFT

RICKSHAW

ROCKET

SKATES

SKIS

SLEDGE

SNO-CAT

SNOWMOBILE

SPACECRAFT

TANK

TAXI

TRAIN

TRAM

TRAP

TRAVOIS

TROIKA

VAN

WAGON

```
S K I S L E D G E A B E T A
E L I N E R V N S R O Y T E
R A T O I R A H C N A F R M
I S T W A L N G A O T G A A
C P F M P D O C L B A H I R
K A A O S N O C A T G C N T
S C R B D I L O T U R G H T
H E L I N E L G O N D O L A
A C O L U N A R R O V E R L
W R R E E S B B I C Y C L E
B A R G E T R A V O I S Y N
A F Y T E T A U T O G Y R O
T T A I B E B I L A N O R G
S K R X O K U A R A N L E A
S K O A R C S A T S F K F W
O R E T P O C I L E H S B E
F R E J T R O I K A L I F T
S J B A C I D E P L Y U P W
```

Down the Line

Without measuring, can you say which is the longer of
these two sleepers resting on the railway lines?

On the Beach

The picture below shows a typical British family relaxing on the beach. Underneath that is the same picture—or is it? In fact there are ten subtle differences between the two. Can you spot what they are?

Follow the Signal

The railway signal box panel at the top of the picture has four buttons on it (if you are clever you have already noticed that). Can you follow the cables to see which button you would have to press to operate the signal?

Happy Landings

Can you guess in which country you would be if you landed at these airports?

JOHN F. KENNEDY
GANDER
DUM DUM
HEATHROW
SCHIPHOL
TEMPELHOF
FORNEBU
SHEREMETYEVO
KAI TAK
ORLY
BROMMA
LEONARDO DA VINCI
KINGSFORD SMITH
PALISADOES

Road Traveller's Quiz

1. What cars in Britain do not have registration number plates?

2. By what name is the Gravelly Hill interchange on the M6 motorway near Birmingham better known?

3. What do the letters TIR on a lorry mean?

4. Who invented 'cat's eyes'?

5. What is a CD plate?

6. All cars over three years old have to have an annual vehicle test, the M.O.T. test. What do the intials M.O.T. stand for?

7. The symbols of the motoring organizations RAC and AA are familiar on British roads. Do you know what the initials stand for in each case?

8. What is an odometer?

9. What road sign shows the shapes of a black car and a red car surrounded by a red ring?

10. What is a toll bridge?

What cars in Britain do not have registration number plates?

stolen ones

Emblems of the Air

If your travels take you to an international airport you will see lots of aeroplanes (No! You do surprise me! It is amazing what you can learn from a book like this).

Most airlines have their own special insignia (posh name for a badge or emblem) on their planes. Some are shown on this page. See if you can name the different airlines shown and the countries from which they come.

Four Little Words

If you are lucky enough to travel abroad (no, not one of the Norfolk Broads—foreign countries) it is useful, and good manners, to know some of the language. It's not necessary to know a lot because you can often get by if you point to things you want, or do a mime. The only problems come when you want something like a sausage sandwich covered in custard. How on earth do you mime that? (Answers on a postcard, please).

All you really need in a foreign country (apart from this book, money, sun tan oil, passport, tummy bug medicine, radio, clothes, a Union Jack and a twenty ton truck to carry everything) is the ability to say four little words—hello, goodbye, please and thank you.

They will not take a whizzkid like you very long to learn. And to save you the trouble of looking them up, some are given here. (The words in brackets are a rough English version of how you should pronounce the words).

	hello	*goodbye*
FRENCH	bonjour	au revoir
	(*bon sure*)	(*oh rev-wah*)
SPANISH	hola	adios
	(*oh-la*)	(*add-ee-os*)
GERMAN	Guten Tag	Auf Wiedersehn
	(*gooten tak*)	(*owf veeder-sane*)
ITALIAN	buon giorno	a rivederci
	(*boo-on jorno*)	(*ah river-dare-chee*)
DUTCH	hallo	tot ziens
	(*hullo*)	(*tot zeens*)
PORTUGUESE	ola	adeus
	(*oh-la*)	(*add-eh-oosh*)

please	thank you
s'il vous plait	merci
(sea voo play)	*(mer-si)*
por favor	gracias
(por fab-or)	*(grath-ee-yas)*
Bitte	Danke
(bitter)	*(danker)*
per favore	grazie
(pair favor-eh)	*(grat-see-eh)*
alstublieft	dank u
(ul-stoo-bleeft)	*(dunk-oo)*
por favor	obrigado (men)
	obrigada (women)
(por fav-or)	*(obree-gah-doo/da)*

More Signs of the Times

Here are some mixed-up road signs. Can you say what each sign is really for?

1 Tea bar ahead

2 Hammer and nails on road

3 You are on a race course

4 Croquet prohibited

5 Speed limit 1,000 mph

6. Bad weather (Thunder and Lightning)

7 Beware of tuning forks

Odds and Ends

Here are some more unusual facts and stories about travel that you can pass on to your fellow passengers to cheer them up:

A tip from Charles Dudley Warner, nineteenth century American writer: "In making up a party for a travelling excursion, always be sure to include one ignorant person who will ask all the questions you are ashamed to ask, and you will acquire a great deal of information you would otherwise lose."

Excuse me Can you recommend a good lunatic asylum near here?

Always be sure to include one ignorant person who will ask the questions you are ashamed to.

The first passengers in a hot air balloon designed by the Montgolfier brothers in 1873 were a sheep, a cock and a duck.

In 1985 two girls travelled five hundred miles because they wanted to go to the toilet. They boarded a train in Carlisle for the sole purpose of using the loo. But the train started and didn't stop until it reached Milton Keynes. It cost the girls £57—an expensive way to spend a penny.

Crows once brought the fast bullet trains of Japan to a standstill. The birds had built their nests on the electric pylons and this caused short circuits. The Japanese engineers had to treat the pylons with bird repellant to prevent any further stoppages.

A Boeing 747 jumbo jet is so long (225 feet) that the whole of the first powered flight could have taken place in one (if it had been invented then, of course). The flight, made by the Wright brothers in 1903, was 120 feet so there would be plenty of room in the jumbo.

According to the law, London taxi drivers should carry a bale of hay at all times. The law dates back to the days of horse-drawn cabs and has never been changed. It is also necessary for them to carry a bucket and a shovel to collect any droppings!

Jokes on Wheels

POLICEMAN: Hey, you shouldn't be crossing the road in this dangerous spot. Can't you see there's a zebra crossing just up the road?
PEDESTRIAN: Well, I hope he's having better luck than me.

When Bert Thostlewink took his car to the garage for an oil change the car was in such a bad state that they advised him to keep the oil and change the car.

The best time to buy a used car is when it's new.

MR SMITH: Why have you got two 'L' plates on the front of your car?
MR JONES: Oh, one is for the wife—she's learning to drive. The other is for her mother—she's learning to be a back seat driver.

According to statistics one man is run down every thirty seconds in London—and he's getting rather fed up with it.

DRIVER: Are my car indicators working?
DOPEY DICK: Yes, no, yes, no, yes, no . . .

Which driver never commits a traffic offence?
A screwdriver.

Why did the man drive over the cliff?
He wanted to test his air brakes.

Why did the man drive his car into the river?
He wanted to dip his headlights.

Where is the best place for a motorist to get refreshment?
At a T junction.

What noise does a cat make going down the motorway?
Miaooooooooooooooooow.

Where do Volkswagens go when they get old and worn?
The Old Volks Home.

What has one horn and gives milk?
A milk lorry.

What did the traffic warden say after booking several motorists for illegal parking?
I've done a fine day's work.

What did the traffic warden have in his sandwiches?
Traffic jam.

What's a juggernaut?
An empty beer mug.

What did the broken car horn say?
I don't give a hoot.

When is a car not a car?
When it turns into a lay-by.

DRIVER: Could you tell me the way to Bath?
POLICEMAN: Well, I always use soap and water.

FIRST ANGEL: It looks as if Charlie was a careful motorist when he was on earth.
SECOND ANGEL: What makes you say that?
FIRST ANGEL: Because as soon as he arrived up here he asked to be fitted with wing mirrors.

It is said that we are in the space age. If you have ever tried to park a car in a city centre you will know how silly that is.

TEACHER: State the number of cars made in Britain in any one year.
PUPIL: 1066—none.

MOTORIST: When I bought this car you said it was rust free but the bodywork is rotting away with it.
DEALER: That's right, the car was rust free. We didn't charge you for it.

Bet You Didn't Know

Lhasa Airport in Tibet is the highest airport in the world.

A survey has shown that over seventy per cent of damage to passengers' luggage on air journeys is the result of overpacking.

The world's first airline stewardess was a nurse called Ellen Church who made her first official flight between San Francisco, California, and Cheyenne, Wyoming, on 15th May, 1930.

The world's first airline stewardess was a nurse....

On 4th October, 1958 a de Havilland Comet 4 started the first transatlantic jet passenger service.

On 25th August, 1919 a de Havilland DH16 flew from Hounslow in England to Le Bourget, France to start the first daily international commercial airline service. There were four passengers, the flight took 2½ hours and the fare was £21 for the one-way crossing.

Winston Churchill became the first British Prime Minister to make a transatlantic flight when, on 16–17th January, 1942, he flew between Bermuda and Plymouth.

Concorde was the first supersonic aeroplane to carry passengers on regular scheduled services. The service started on 21st January, 1976 when simultaneous take-offs were made by British Airways Concorde 206 from London to Bahrain and Air France's 205 from Paris to Rio de Janeiro.

The first aeroplane to be fitted with a lavatory was the *Russky Vitiaz*, a giant Russian passenger transport plane which was first flown in 1913. Very practical people, the Russians!

Sign Language

It can make a pleasant break during a long car journey to stop for a picnic lunch. Great if the weather is fine but Dad always seems to stop just as it is about to pour with rain. You all get out and traipse into a nearby field. As you walk through the thigh-high stinging nettles you can hear the ants sharpening their knives and forks, getting ready to eat your food. At last you spot a suitable site. At the same time you sight a suitable spot.

You are about to unpack all the goodies when someone points out a sign that says you can go no further. While the rest of the family are arguing about what to do next you mentally rearrange the letters of the sign into a more sensible message and one that is more usual in the circumstances. The sign is pictured below. *What other message can you make from the letters?*

Fun on the Move

There are lots and lots (in fact there are even more than that) of games that you can play to while away the time on a journey. Provided that they do not distract the driver or pilot (playing tag on aeroplane wings is definitely out) fun games are best. Miserable games are just . . . well . . . miserable. All the games in this section are fun to play, so let's get on with it without further delay.

Traveller's Hide and Seek

All you need for this game is a brain. Oh, no! You haven't left it at home have you? Well, you'd better go and get it—and don't leave it behind again!

A game of hide and seek in a car or other vehicle? Sounds impossible, doesn't it? It is quite difficult to squeeze yourself into the glove compartment. And if you try hiding in the ashtray your feet will stick out so someone is bound to spot you. That's the worst of having big feet.

So, how do you play hide and seek on a journey? It's quite simple—all you need is a brain. And as you've got a simple brain you'll be very good at this.

One player, the hider, simply imagines where he or she would like to hide. The other players, the seekers, have to guess where it is. It's that simple!

To keep the game reasonably short the seekers are allowed to ask the hider only 25 questions in an attempt to discover the hiding place. And, to be fair to the seekers the hider can only hide in a hidey-hole (hidey-hi!) in which he or she could normally hide.

It is also a good idea (especially with younger players) to limit the hiding places to places that the players actually know. So, it is quite all right for you to hide in Granny's cupboard under the stairs (assuming it is big enough and you are not scared of the dark) but it is a bit unfair on the others if you decide to hide in Great Snoring Zoo inside the left nostril of an Indian elephant!

Parking Tickets

This is a game for two players in a car travelling through a town. One player looks through a window on one side of the car and the other player looks out on the other side.

At a given signal (the driver can give this) each player starts counting the cars parked on his or her side of the road. After a certain length of time (the driver, another passenger, or maybe your own watch can tell you when time is up) the two players announce how many cars they spotted. The one with the highest number is, of course, the winner.

Only cars parked at the side of the road are to be included in this game. Moving cars do not count (which is not surprising for cars cannot count, anyway!).

Squiggles

Nobody loses in this game. But, on the other hand, no-one wins either for it is played simply for fun (as should all games, really).

One player draws a simple squiggle on a piece of paper. Another player then has to add some more lines to make the squiggle into a proper drawing.

Don't know what a squiggle is? Shame on you—they are delicious fried in a little butter and served on a bed of fresh lettuce with a pile of chips. (What is he rambling on about?)

These are typical squiggles:

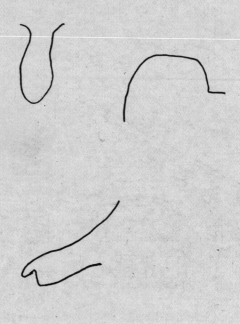

When the second player has finished the three squiggles become beautiful works of art (well almost!) like these:

WORKS OF ART
by P. Squiggles

PORTRAIT OF MY
FATHER. P. SQUIGGLES

MUMS NEW CAR

BIG GAME
by P. Squiggles

All my own Squiggles

Get the idea?

If you are presented with a squiggle that looks difficult to turn into a picture, try turning the paper around and look at it from different angles. There is nothing in the rules to stop you—in fact, there are no rules at all—which makes them easy to remember!

Squiggles are a bit of fun—as all travel games should be. It makes the journey far less boring if you can have a giggle with a squiggle!

Number Frustration

Each player takes a sheet of paper and writes the numbers from one to twenty on it. The numbers should be scattered all over the sheet at random (Random is a village about three miles from here—turn left at the traffic lights). A circle is drawn around each number.

Once you have done that, you do it all over again! (Isn't this exciting?) Scatter another set of numbers from one to twenty on the same sheet and draw circles around them.

The players now swop papers. The object of the game is to draw a line joining up each pair of the same number. When putting in these 'joining' lines you are not allowed to cross any line you have already drawn. The person who joins most pairs of numbers is the winner.

As the numbers do not have to be paired in numerical order it takes some thought to decide which ones to join up first. If you pick the wrong pairs you can block yourself from joining up some of the other numbers. It can be very frustrating!

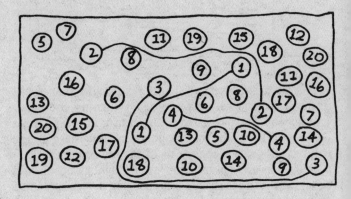

Dear Auntie Joan

A long journey always seems to go quicker if you can have a laugh or two (or three). *Dear Auntie Joan* is the game to give you lots of laughs en route (I wonder what that means!).

Each of the players but one are handed slips of paper. On each slip they have to write a question. The question should be a bit like those sent to 'agony aunts' in magazines and newspapers. Questions such as:

What shall I do about Uncle Harry?
How do you know when you are in love?
What's the best cure for the screaming habdabs?
*What's the best way to remove strawberry stains from frilly
  knickers?*

The player who is not writing questions writes a number of possible answers on separate slips of paper. The player does not yet know, of course, what the questions are going to be. Some of the answers might be:

Boil in warm soap suds and then iron.
Put in a hot oven for half an hour.
Stand in the garden for ten minutes.
Give the kiss of life.

All the questions slips are folded, put in a bag and then shaken up. The answer slips are also folded and put into another bag.

Someone reaches into the question bag and takes out a slip of paper. A slip is also removed from the answer bag and both are then read out. It is quite amazing the crazy answers you can get to equally strange questions when you consult Auntie Joan.

You'll end up with something like this:

QUESTION: *Where can I get straight bananas?*

ANSWER: *Plant garlic around your roses.*

Or:

QUESTION: *How can I cure a bunion?*

ANSWER: *Stuff it with currants and cover with hot lemon sauce.*

Question. HOW CAN I CURE A BUNION?

Answer. Stuff it with currants and cover it with hot lemon sauce.

Traffic Jam

The pictures on this page show a typical scene on British roads—a traffic jam, with cars tailing back as far as the eye can see. If you are stuck in a traffic jam (or a traffic marmalade) you can while away the time by looking at these two pictures for, although they appear to be the same, there are ten slight differences between them. Can you spot them?

Bus Laughs

What form of transport is safest in a thunderstorm?
A bus, because it has a conductor.

How do you feel if you are run over by a bus?
Tyred.

Why did the man become a bus conductor?
So he could tell people where to get off.

The ticket inspector boarded the bus and began checking the tickets. When he asked one lady she had hers but did not have a ticket for her son. "I'm sorry, inspector," she said, "but I am afraid that my son has eaten his ticket. What shall I do?"

The inspector pondered the problem for a while and then he said: "I suggest, madam, that you buy him a second helping."

Do the buses run on time?
Usually, yes.
No, they don't. They run on wheels!

Do you know that all the buses are stopping today?
No, I didn't. Why is that?
To let the passengers off.

What did the traffic lights say to the bus?
Don't look now, I'm changing.

LADY PASSENGER: Excuse me, conductor. Am I all right for the zoo?
CONDUCTOR: Judging by the look of you, yes. But I'm a bus conductor not a zoologist.

Circadian Dysrhythmia

Circadian dysrhythmia? "What on earth is that?" you may ask. And even if you don't ask, I am going to tell you anyway because I've just looked it up in the dictionary. (Useful things, dictionaries—it's the one place where Thursday comes before Wednesday and success comes before work).

Circadian dysrhythmia is the technical name for jetlag, a symptom of modern jet air travel. So, now you know.

But what is jetlag?

The human body has its own built-in clock (now you know why that cuckoo pops out of your mouth every hour). This clock tells you when to go to bed, when to get up, when to have meals and lots of other things as well (bet you always thought it was just your mother who told you when to do such things). In some mysterious way this clock keeps time with the earth and the sun.

Everything runs smoothly until you start jetting across the world. If, for example, you fly by plane (that's the best way to fly) from London to New York you can leave London at 10.30 am and arrive in New York at 8.30 am local time—two hours before you started! You know that it is 8.30 but your body clock is still in tune (now it's musical!) with the time back home. It takes quite a while for the body to sort itself out. In fact it has been proved scientifically that it takes one day for the body to recover for each hour of time change.

This means that on a long journey west it can take up to four days for the body to get back to normal. Travelling east is even worse for there can be anything up to five hours time difference and it can take at least a week for the body to readjust—by which time you are probably on your way back home and the whole thing starts all over again!

Cars from the Country

When a car travels abroad it has to bear a plate that indicates from which country it has come. British cars, for example, have a GB plate when they are taken overseas. Next time you are out on the road see how many different plates you can spot. The plates usually consist of letters so here is a list of some of them to help you identify the country of origin.

A	Austria	DK	Denmark
AUS	Australia	DZ	Algeria
B	Belgium	E	Spain
BG	Bulgaria	ET	Egypt
BR	Brazil	F	France
BUR	Burma	FL	Liechtenstein
C	Cuba	GB	Great Britain &
CDN	Canada		Northern Ireland
CH	Switzerland	GCA	Guatemala
CO	Colombia	GR	Greece
CS	Czechoslovakia	H	Hungary
CY	Cyprus	I	Italy
D	West Germany	IL	Israel

IND	India	R	Romania
IR	Iran	RA	Argentina
IRL	Eire	RC	China
IRQ	Iraq	RCH	Chile
IS	Iceland	RH	Haiti
J	Japan	RI	Indonesia
JOR	Jordan	RIM	Mauritania
L	Luxemburg	RL	Lebanon
MA	Morocco	RSM	San Marino
MC	Monaco	S	Sweden
MEX	Mexico	SF	Finland
N	Norway	SGP	Singapore
NIC	Nicaragua	SU	Russia
NL	Netherlands	SYR	Syria
NZ	New Zealand	T	Thailand
P	Portugal	TN	Tunisia
PA	Panama	TR	Turkey
PAK	Pakistan	U	Uruguay
PE	Peru	USA	United States
PI	Philippines		of America
PL	Poland	YU	Yugoslavia
PY	Paraguay	ZA	South Africa

Flights of Fancy

Although Sir William Cayley expounded the principles of flight in 1809, many aspiring (not perspiring) inventors chose to ignore the ideas he had laid down. As a result there were a lot of rather crazy designs for flying machines around at the end of the nineteenth century.

As the bicycle was a popular form of transport at the time a number of inventors decided that pedal power would be a good way to propel a flying machine. The designs ranged from a simple overhead propellor attached to pedals to extremely complicated machines filled with compressed air to make them lighter.

Dr. W.O. Ayres devised a flying machine in 1885 that looked rather like a climbing frame or a four poster bed. Its main source of power was compressed air which powered two propellers. Two other propellers were powered by pedals. In addition to pedalling, the poor pilot also had to turn a wheel with his right hand to operate a vertical propeller that provided the forward movement of the machine. The inventor believed that the machine was definitely capable of flight—but it was never built.

Birds were the inspiration for a lot of the early designs. Many ideas were put forward that used flapping wings to get the vehicle airborne. Joseph Kaufmann of Glasgow was one person who thought that this was feasible and he actually demonstrated such a machine in 1869. Unfortunately the whole thing collapsed and so did Kaufmann's dreams of becoming one of the pioneers of aviation.

A contributor to the *Scientific American* magazine in 1865 also used birds as his inspiration. He reasoned that as eagles were known to carry off lambs, ten eagles should have sufficient power to lift a man. He devised a circular framework of hollow tubes which supported a basket for the pilot to sit in. Ten eagles were to be fitted with jackets and attached to the framework. The birds were to be controlled by a system of cords running through the tubes. Luckily for the birds this idea was never tried out.

You're on Your Own

If you are travelling on your own and you want something to occupy your mind here are a few games to try:

Transformations
Think of two words that have the same number of letters. Now try to change the first word into the second word by altering one letter at a time. But each time you change a letter a proper word has to be formed. The object of the game is to make the transformation in as few steps as possible. If, for example, the two words you choose are 'map' and 'toe' the stages might be map, tap, top, toe.

You will probably find it best to start with three-letter words. When you can do these try using longer words.

Words from Words

For this game you take any word of seven or more letters and then try to make as many words as possible from the word you've chosen. So, from the word 'transport', for example, you can get words such as post, roast, strap, sort, rant, pant, star and many others.

Single Handed Snap

Take a pack of cards and give them a good shuffle. Turn over cards from the top of the pack one at a time. As you do so you count to yourself—ace, two, three, four . . . through to the king, then start again. If you turn over a card of the same value as the number you are counting you remove it from the pack.

When you have been all through the pack simply start all over again.

The object of the game is to remove as many cards as possible. It sometimes happens that you can go all the way through the cards without any of them matching. If that happens you have lost the game—hard luck!

On the Road

A lot of road maps are confusing, but none is more confusing than that of the little town of Getlostin. A map of the town is shown below. See if you can find a route from south to north through the town as if you were travelling from Fugglewick Heath to Wrigglesworth. And the best of luck!

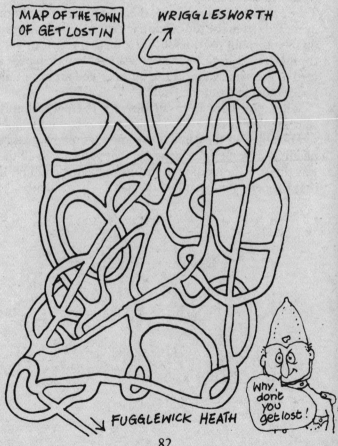

How Strange Can You Get?

Over the years people have undertaken some very strange journeys and used some most unusual methods of travelling. Perhaps one of the strangest journeys of all time was that of the Reverend Geoffrey Howard in 1975. Partly to raise money for charity, but also because it had never been done before, he set out to push a wheelbarrow across the Sahara Desert!

The wheelbarrow he used was nothing like the ordinary garden version for it had been specially designed by the engineering department of a college at Oxford University. It had an enormous central wheel—and a sail to help it along. The parson planned to cover the 3,200 km journey across the burning sands in a hundred days. In fact he covered the distance in six days less than this in spite of the fact that during the journey his tent caught fire, burning some of his essential supplies, and the wheel broke so he had to repair it as best he could.

Wheels of another sort were used by Dennis Wickham when he travelled from London to Australia in 1970/71. He made the whole journey by bicycle. He started from London on 31st March, 1970, crashed in Berlin, was arrested in Bulgaria and he was stoned in Turkey, but eventually arrived, more or less unscathed, in Brisbane on 1st November, 1971. But the most amazing thing about his journey was the bike he used—an 1872 solid-rubber-tyred penny-farthing! He did cheat a little, however—on the occasions when there was a good strong tail wind he used his umbrella as a sail!

Roller skates were the mode of transport favoured by Theodore James Coombs in 1979. He travelled from Los Angeles to New York and then back to Yates Centre, Kansas, a distance of 8,357 km (5,193 miles). It took him 107 days to make the round trip.

In 1891 Sylvain Dornon walked from Paris to Moscow via Vilno, a distance of 2,945 km (1,830 miles). He did the walk in a number of stages over a period of 58 days. Nothing particularly remarkable in that you may think—there certainly would not be if the walk was ordinary. But Sylvain was not satisfied with being conventional so he made the entire journey on stilts!

But the most unusual traveller of all time must be the Texan, Plennie Wingo. On 15th April, 1931, he set off from Santa Monica, California. A year and a half later he arrived in Istanbul, Turkey. He had travelled a distance of 12,875 kilometres and he had walked all the way—backwards!

Channel Crossings

Tens of thousands of travellers cross the English Channel every year. Most of them are journeying to a holiday destination or returning home from a holiday; many are travelling for business reasons; and some are crossing the Channel just for the fun of it.

The fun travellers have tried all manner of weird and wonderful ways of crossing from coast to coast. Some have succeeded but many more have failed in their attempts. They have tried making the journey on rafts, skis, air mattresses, cars, bicycles (believe it or not) and one intrepid traveller actually drifted across on a bale of hay—how corny!

One person, Bob Platten, has probably tried more whacky Channel crossings than anyone else. His many forms of transport have included a giant leather shoe, an enormous gin bottle, a 9ft long barrel and a motorized bedstead—no doubt his sleep came in *waves* that night.

In 1977, three soldiers floated across to France in a bathroom suite, consisting of a bath, basin and toilet, affixed to a motorized raft. It took them about ten hours to make the crossing and they were *flushed* with success.

Many people have actually managed to swim the Channel. The most famous person to do this is undoubtedly the first—Matthew Webb. It took Webb, a merchant navy captain, 21 hours 45 minutes to swim from Dover to Calais in 1875. The tide drove him back and he had to swim an estimated 61 kilometres (38 miles) to make the 33 km (21 miles) crossing. Fifty one years later Gertrude Caroline Erdele from America became the first woman to swim the Channel. She swam from Cap Gris-Nez in France to Deal, England in 14 hours and 39 minutes.

Five months before Matthew Webb's epic feat, Captain Paul Boynton had made a similar crossing. But, unlike Webb, Boynton did not swim unaided, for the purpose of his trip was to demonstrate the efficiency of his newly-invented life-saving suit. The suit was made of rubber and inflated. There was a tiny sail built into one of the feet so all Boynton had to do was lie on his back and paddle. He was even able to enjoy a good cigar on the way!

Another person who used the Channel to demonstrate a particular idea was S. F. Cody in 1903. He wanted to prove that the Channel could be a useful aerial observation post in wartime. To publicize his idea he built a boat that was powered by a kite. Although he managed to make the crossing it took him a very long time to do so. On the way across he was almost hit by a passing steamer, then he hit the treacherous Goodwin Sands—and then the wind changed direction and he started being towed back to France so he had to haul down the kite and use it as a sail until he made his eventual arrival at Dover.

Nowadays many people fly the Channel but the first people to do so were Jean-Pierre Blanchard and Dr. John Jeffries in 1785. They made the crossing in a hydrogen–filled balloon—but they almost didn't make it. The balloon began to lose height towards the end of the journey, and they had to take off almost all their clothes to lighten the load. As the flight was made in January they must have been rather cold when they eventually landed in the Forêt de Felmores in France.

Louis Bleriot did not fare much better when he made the first aeroplane crossing in 1909 for he crash-landed in a field near Dover Castle. But it must be said that he was not feeling very well at the time as he had had a nasty accident a few days before. His leg had been badly burned but he was still determined to make the historic flight. "I may not be able to walk," he said, "but I can still fly." And that is exactly what he did!

When Is the Next Bus?

When the people of Puzzlitout travel they like to go by bus. This is because they are keen on puzzles and so is the local bus owner Al Fairzpleez. The bus timetables in Puzzlitout are not like normal bus timetables. A typical example is given below. See if you can follow the clues and work out the order in which the ten buses will leave the bus station.

The bus to Frampton Wick is the fourth to leave the bus station.

Seven buses leave the station before the one for Sloopytown.

The bus for Failestown goes after the bus for Colesthroop.

Windy Boggles is the destination of the bus that leaves just before the bus to Frampton Wick.

The Failestown bus is followed by the bus to Grumbleford.

The bus for Crockville goes out after the bus for Ormigrigg but before the bus to Windy Boggles.

Grumbleford is the destination of the bus three places ahead of the bus to Upther Hill.

The bus for Eggsanham used to be the seventh to leave the bus station but it now goes out two buses later.

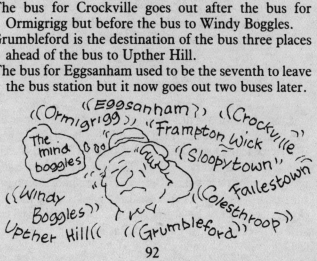

Would You Believe It?

A lady, driving from Sydney to Melbourne in Australia, made a wrong turning and drove into a tunnel. The tunnel was rather long and after two miles of twisting and turning the car ran out of petrol. As it was very dark in the tunnel the lady decided to stay where she was until someone came along. Eventually someone did—three miners on their way to work. She had driven into a coal mine!

If walking is your favourite form of travel try walking at a steady pace non-stop for a year. If you managed to do it you would have travelled a distance equal to the circumference of the earth—but you'd be feeling fairly worn out and your feet would be fraying at the edges!

The Forth railway bridge (whatever happened to the first, second and third?) is a metre longer in the summer than it is in the winter.

Motorists are often concerned about how many miles their car does to a gallon of petrol. Whatever the answer they should be lucky they don't drive the QE2 for a gallon of fuel is only enough to move this ocean liner five centimetres!

Jacques Loti doesn't ride bicycles—he eats them! Under the name of Monsieur Mangetout (Mr. Eat-all) he first saws the bike into pieces and then enjoys a great meal. He admits that he doesn't enjoy eating the brakes because they have a tendency to get stuck in the throat. His favourite part is the chain because "it is nice and greasy and has the best taste". You've heard of 'meals on wheels' but with Mr Mangetout it's a case of 'wheels are meals'.

Transports of Delight

Man (and woman) has always been an inventor. But sometimes the inventions have turned out to be a little bit unusual and occasionally absolutely crazy. Some of the peculiar forms of transport that have been devised over the years have also been rather strange. Many ideas were never actually tried—like the large ball-like contraption devised by a French bicycle manufacturer in 1884.

The device consisted of a large globe about two metres in diameter made in a transparent material. Inside the ball was an iron shaft with a seat mounted at its centre. At each end of the shaft iron balls would rotate in socket joints and press against the sides of the sphere.

To get into this strange decide there was to be a small door which when closed would lie flush along the surface of the globe. Once inside the rider propelled himself by walking along the wall of the sphere!

It was claimed that the vehicle would be equally as effective on water as on land but it was never made.

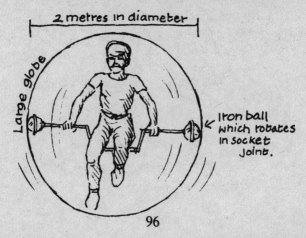

At about the same time an American invented the 'pedispeed', a type of roller skate. The pedispeed consisted of two wheels, one for each foot, attached to the legs. The inventor admitted that some practice was needed to skate along on these wheels but that once the skill was acquired it provided "a delightful, healthful and graceful pastime at all seasons of the year." One thing the inventor forgot to include on his ingenious invention was a brake—presumably if you wanted to stop you simply crashed into a tree!

THE AMAZING AMERICAN PEDISPEED

A delightful, healthful and graceful pastime at all seasons of the year

(some practice needed)

One invention of this period that was actually tested was the 'Zimmer Boat', named after its inventor. It was powered by a pedal-operated propeller fixed either beneath or at the stern of the boat. In front of the driver was a large handlebar which controlled two floats, one on each side, which could be adjusted to avoid loss of balance. It was claimed that the Zimmer Boat had been tested in rough weather and that it could go faster than any rowing boat.

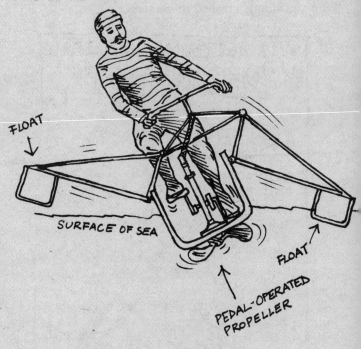

FLOAT

SURFACE OF SEA

FLOAT

PEDAL-OPERATED PROPELLER

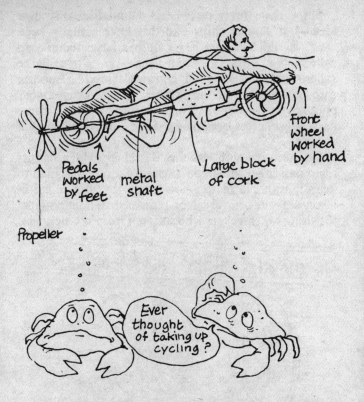

Another form of water transport was a floating bicycle. It consisted of a large block of cork through the centre of which was a metal shaft. A wheel at the front of the shaft and pedals at the other end were used to turn a propeller. A swimmer lay on the cork and by working the front wheel with his hands and the pedals with his feet travelled through the water. William A. Richardson, the inventor of this sea-going cycle, claimed that this device would enable anyone to swim effectively without any previous practice and that it was possible to attain a speed of up to six miles an hour.

Ships that travel on wheels sound like a strange idea—but several ships like this have actually been used. In 1882 Robert Fryer built a large steam ship called the 'Alice' which ran on three large rollers—rather like an overgrown tricycle. Another ship on wheels was the 'Svanen' which proved very popular in Denmark where it was used to carry passengers across two lakes and the intervening stretch of land.

One unusual ship was the 'Bessemer' which had its main passenger saloon on a series of levers designed to keep it still. No matter how much the ship rolled in heavy seas the central saloon remained stationary—just the thing for travellers who suffered from sea-sickness.

BESSEMER FIRST CLASS

But such strange vehicles do not only belong to the nineteenth century. There have been quite a few in this century as well. One of the most unusual is the 'Rollracer' which consists of two giant tractor wheels with a seat positioned between them. Milutin Dragic, a Swedish restaurant owner, built the car and he claims that it is a lot safer than ordinary cars. He says that it cannot skid, even in the wettest of weather and that it can make a perfect right angle turn even when travelling at high speed. The seat is designed so that it swings to and fro and this absorbs any impact if the vehicle crashes. If the crash is particularly severe the central portion revolves right over. That must be pretty scary!

ROLLRACER

Giant tractor wheels

Transparent shields

Seat is designed to swing to and fro

Puzzles for Passengers

Next time you go on a long journey have a go at these puzzles. They will help the time go by much more quickly.

Up the Pole
Imagine that you have just completed a long journey and you have arrived at the North Pole. You now decide to travel on to Russia. In which direction, north, south, east, or west, would you have to travel to get there?

Cross Purposes
A farmer is travelling to market with his dog, a hen and a bag of corn. At one point he has to cross a river by boat but there is only enough room in the boat for one object. This poses quite a problem for if he takes the corn and leaves the dog and the hen together the dog will eat the hen. And if he leaves the hen and the corn together at any time the hen will eat the corn. How can he get all three items across safely?

Up in the Air

Charlie Bogglewrack, Fred Beephburger and Hortense Bumbletum all board an aeroplane at Heathrow. The stewardess shows them to their seats. Charlie sits at the back of the aircraft, Fred is seated towards the front of the plane and Hortense prefers to be at the centre. When everyone is comfortable the pilot boards, speaks to each of the passengers in turn and wishes them all a good trip before taking his place in the cockpit. The plane then sets off for New York. During the flight the passengers are served with a meal after which the stewardess brings them all a cup of coffee. Eventually, after an uneventful journey, the plane lands at New York. Of all the people on the plane who has travelled the furthest distance?

All Change

The picture on this page is of a railway siding in which there is an engine, a tanker truck and a carriage. The engine driver has to shunt the tanker across to position C and the carriage over to position B. The length of track marked D is long enough to take either the tanker or the carriage. It is too short to take the engine. How does the engine driver manage to change the positions of the tanker and the carriage?

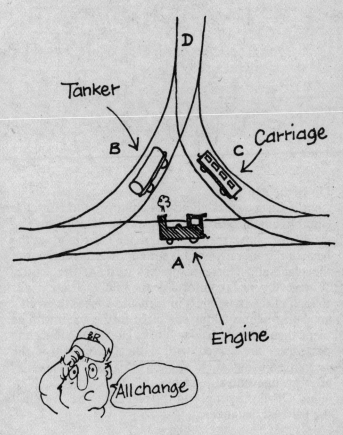

Train of Thought

An Inter City express train sets off from Edinburgh at two minutes past two and travels to London at an average speed of sixty miles an hour. At twenty minutes past three another train leaves London bound for Edinburgh. This train's average speed is seventy miles an hour. Which train is furthest from London when the two trains meet? The distance from Edinburgh to London is four hundred miles.

Play on Words

See if you can work out the well-known phrase or saying hidden in the items on this page. To give you some idea of how it works take a look at the first one, the name 'Macbeth' on top of 'words'. Macbeth, as you of course know, is a play by Shakespeare so the answer is 'Play on Words'—get it?

Once you get the idea you will find that it is great fun to make up your own puzzles like this. You could then use them to perplex your family and friends on long journeys.

You've been told what the first one is, now see if you can decipher the rest. You will find the answers on page 111.

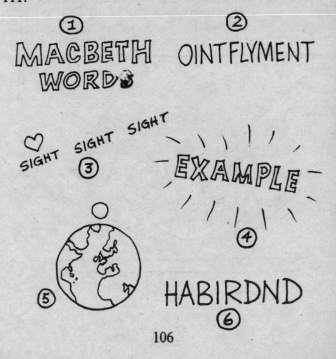

Answers to Puzzles

FOOD FOR THOUGHT: Spaghetti Bolognese = Italy; Roganjosh = India; Paella = Spain; Smorgasbord = Denmark; Cous-Cous = North Africa; Goulash = Hungary; Wiener Schnitzel = Austria; Bird's Nest Soup = China; Sauerkraut = Germany; Haggis = Scotland; Tamale = Mexico; Shish Kebab = Turkey; Dolmas = Greece; Borscht = Russia.

LOST PROPERTY: Umbrella; Camera; Suitcase; Overcoat; Magazine; Handbag; False Teeth; Walking Stick; Haversack; Wooden Leg; Golf Clubs.

ON THE MAP:
1. Orchard; 2. Church (with tower); 3. Windmill; 4. Post Office; 5. Site of a battle; 6. Bus Station; 7. Camp Site; 8. Church (with spire); 9. Youth Hostel; 10. Power lines(pylons).

SIGNS OF THE TIMES: 1. Uneven surface; 2. No right turn; 3. Jetty; 4. Road narrows on both sides; 5. Road works; 6. Slippery surface.

DOWN THE LINE: Both the sleepers are exactly the same length. They look different due to an optical illusion that tricks the eyes into thinking (I didn't know eyes could think!) that the top one looks longer. This illusion is called the Pongo illusion (you may not believe that but it is true!)

TRANSPORT TANGLE:

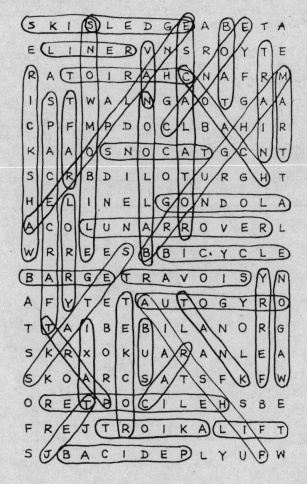

ON THE BEACH: 1. Band on ball; 2. Dot on scarf of girl with icecream; 3. Frill on dress of girl with icecream; 4. Band on boy's hat; 5. Eyebrow on man; 6. Eyebrow on dog on newspaper; 7. Black label on bottle on newspaper; 8. Collar on girl on newspaper; 9. Button on fat woman's dress; 10. Braid on sleeve of fat woman's dress.

FOLLOW THE SIGNAL: Button C operates the signal.

HAPPY LANDINGS: John F. Kennedy = USA (New York); Gander = Canada (Newfoundland); Dum Dum = India (Calcutta); Heathrow = England (London); Schiphol = The Netherlands (Amsterdam); Tempelhof = West Germany (Berlin); Fornebu = Norway (Oslo); Sheremetyevo = USSR (Moscow); Kai Tak = Hong Kong; Orly = France (Paris); Bromma = Sweden (Stockholm); Leonardo da Vinci = Italy (Rome); Kingsford Smith = Australia (Sydney); Palisadoes = Jamaica (Kingston).

ROAD TRAVELLER'S QUIZ: 1. Cars that belong to Her Majesty the Queen: 2. Spaghetti Junction; 3. Touring Internationale Routier; 4. Percy Shaw—the first were installed on the roads in 1934; 5. A number plate bearing the letters CD. CD stands for Corps Diplomatique and if a vehicle bears such a plate it usually means that it belongs to an embassy or a consolate; 6. Ministry of Transport; 7. Royal Automobile Club and Automobile Association; 8. It is the device in a motor vehicle that measures the distance travelled; 9. No overtaking; 10. A bridge for which a fee has to be paid before a vehicle is allowed to cross it.

EMBLEMS OF THE AIR: 1. Air Canada, Canada; 2. Japan Air Lines, Japan; 3. Aer Lingus, Eire; 4. South African Airways, Republic of South Africa; 5. Qantas, Australia; 6. British Caledonian Airways, Great Britain.

MORE SIGNS OF THE TIMES: 1. T-junctions; 2. Level crossing; 3. Wild horses and ponies; 4. No U-turns; 5. Weight limit ten tons; 6. Electricity pylons 7. End of dual carriageway.

SIGN LANGUAGE: No Trespassing Allowed.

TRAFFIC JAM: 1. Button on Express truck driver's jacket; 2. Mouth of driver; 3. Cap of driver; 4. Band on hat of driver of first car in centre lane; 5. Headlamps on Freds lorry; 6. Name of Freds lorry; 7. Eyebrows of driver of first car in right-hand lane; 8. Spokes on driving wheel of second car in right-hand lane; 9. Head of driver of third car in right-hand lane; 10. Bands on lamppost.

ON THE ROAD: Did you manage to get from Flugglewick Heath to Wrigglesworth or did you get lost in Getlostin?

WHEN IS THE NEXT BUS?: 1. Ormigrigg; 2. Crockville; 3. Windy Boggles; 4. Frampton Wick; 5. Colesthroop; 6. Failestown; 7. Grumbleford; 8. Sloopytown; 9. Eggsanham; 10. Upther Hill.

PUZZLES FOR PASSENGERS:
Up The Pole. South. No matter where you are going you have to travel south from the North Pole.

Cross Purposes. The farmer takes the hen across first, leaving the dog with the corn. He then goes back and takes the dog across. On the return journey he brings the hen back again. He then leaves the hen and takes the corn across which he leaves with the dog on the opposite bank. For his last trip he goes back and fetches the hen across and all three items are then safely on the other side.

Up in the Air. The stewardess will have travelled the furthest by walking up and down the plane during the flight.

All Change. The engine pushes the carriage up to position D and leaves it there. It then pushes the tanker up to the carriage and the driver couples them together. Both the tanker and the carriage are then pulled down to the left siding and then pushed across to the right. The carriage is left on the right and the tanker is then pushed up to D where it is left for the time being. The engine now pulls the carriage across to the left and then pushes it up to position B. Next the engine goes back across to the right siding then up to C where it pulls the tanker down from D, leaving it at C before returning to its position at A.

Train of Thought. They are both the same distance from London.

PLAY ON WORDS: 1. Play on words; 2. Fly in the ointment; 3. Love at first sight; 4. Shining example; 5. Nothing on Earth; 6. A bird in the hand.

Here are some of the most recent titles in our exciting fiction series:

☐ Journey to Atlantis *J. J. Fortune* £1.75
☐ The Feud in the Chalet School
  Elinor M. Brent-Dyer £1.75
☐ Tomb of Nightmares *J. H. Brennan* £1.95
☐ The Emerald-Eyed Cat Mystery *Carolyn Keene* £1.75
☐ The Demon's Den *Franklin W. Dixon* £1.75
☐ The Mystery of the Kidnapped Whale
  Marc Brandel £1.75
☐ Horse of Fire *Patricia Leitch* £1.75
☐ The Garden of Madness *David Tant* 1.95

Armadas are available in bookshops and newsagents, but can also be ordered by post.

HOW TO ORDER
ARMADA BOOKS, Cash Sales Dept., GPO Box 29, Douglas, Isle of Man, British Isles. Please send purchase price plus 15p per book (maximum postal charge £3.00). Customers outside the UK also send purchase price plus 15p per book. Cheque, postal or money order — no currency.

NAME (Block letters) _____

ADDRESS _____

_____

_____